AUG -- 2022

childsworld.com

Published by The Child's World®
1980 Lookout Drive • Mankato, MN 56003-1705
800-599-READ • www.childsworld.com

Photographs ©: Rob McKay/Shutterstock Images, cover, 1; Gerald Mark Griffin/Shutterstock Images, 2, 9; PJR Photography/Shutterstock Images, 5; Susan E. Viera/Shutterstock Images, 6, 24; Mastak A./Shutterstock Images, 10 (mouse); Shutterstock Images, 10 (owl), 10 (eagle), 10 (falcon), 13, 18, 21; Vladimir Kogan Michael/Shutterstock Images, 14; Georgi Baird/Shutterstock Images, 17

Copyright ©2022 by The Child's World®
All rights reserved. No part of the book may be reproduced or utilized in any form or by any means without written permission from the publisher.

ISBN 9781503849952 (Reinforced Library Binding)
ISBN 9781503850507 (Portable Document Format)
ISBN 9781503851269 (Online Multi-user eBook)
LCCN 2021939874

Printed in the United States of America

ABOUT THE AUTHOR

Marie Pearson is a children's book author who loves animals. Her favorite pastimes are training her dogs and bird-watching. So far, she has spotted eight different raptor species near her home.

CHAPTER ONE
On the Hunt …4

CHAPTER TWO
Benefits of Raptors …8

CHAPTER THREE
Threats and Protections …16

GLOSSARY …22
TO LEARN MORE …23
INDEX …24

On the Hunt

The sky glows deep purple. The sun has just set. A barn owl flies out from its nest on the side of a barn. Its soft feathers help it fly almost silently over the field.

The owl uses its excellent hearing to listen for **prey**. It flies close to the ground. Suddenly, it dives. The bird grabs a pocket gopher with its sharp **talons**. The owl gulps down the entire gopher. That is one less critter to destroy crops in the field.

Barn owls live in most of the United States.

Many people also call raptors birds of prey.

Barn owls are a type of raptor. Raptors are birds that eat meat. Eagles, falcons, hawks, owls, and vultures are all raptors. These birds help keep the number of animals in balance. They help keep the world clean. They also give humans clues when an **ecosystem** is unhealthy. Raptors have a very important role.

Benefits of Raptors

Raptors hunt prey. They have good eyesight. Their talons are strong and sharp. They have a hooked beak. These traits help them catch and eat their food.

Raptors eat many kinds of animals. They eat small mammals, fish, lizards, insects, and smaller birds. Raptors keep these **species** in balance.

Many raptors use their talons or beaks to catch prey.

How Much Food Raptors Eat in a Year

Barn Owl
89 pounds (40 kg) = 1,602 mice

Peregrine Falcon
56 pounds (25 kg) = 1,008 mice

Bald Eagle
292 pounds (132 kg) = 5,256 mice

 = 500 mice; 18 mice in 1 pound (.45 kg)

This graphic shows how many pounds of food some raptors eat in a year. It also shows approximately how many mice that equals. Raptors eat more than just mice, though. Some of the animals they eat are bigger than mice. Others are smaller. A single raptor can eat a lot of pests in a year!

Keeping species numbers in balance keeps ecosystems healthy. If there are too many members of one species, they can eat too much food in an area. They may kill off one type of plant. Then there isn't enough food for other animals. Other animals in the area may starve or leave.

Raptors also help with **pest** control. Rats, gophers, and other animals can spread diseases to people. They can kill crops. These animals also have a lot of **offspring**. When raptors eat them, it lowers the number of pests. They cause fewer problems for people.

Many raptors eat the **remains** of dead animals. Vultures mainly eat dead animals. Other raptors eat dead animals and live prey. This helps keep remains from piling up.

Vultures also keep diseases from spreading. Remains from dead animals can carry diseases. When a vulture eats the remains, the germs die in its stomach. This protects people and other animals.

FUN FACT

Turkey vultures can smell remains from more than 1 mile (1.6 km) away.

Vultures eat the remains of dead animals, called carrion.

Having raptors in an area is a sign the ecosystem is healthy.

Raptors are at the top of the food web. That means no animals eat them. Instead, raptors eat other animals. Many of those animals eat plants.

Raptors are used as a sign of an ecosystem's health. Anything that affects plants and animals lower on the food web affects raptors more. Scientists keep track of raptors. If raptors start disappearing, something may be wrong in the ecosystem. Scientists can figure out what is wrong. They can help the area become healthy again.

Threats and Protections

Raptors face some threats. People use chemicals on plants to kill pests. Those chemicals can also kill raptors. A mouse may get only a small amount of a chemical from the plants it eats. But a hawk eats many mice. It gets that chemical from each mouse it eats.

Habitat loss is also a threat. People destroy natural areas. They bulldoze trees to build cities and make farmland. This causes raptors to lose nesting and hunting grounds.

Some scientists use tags to track raptors. This helps them learn more about the birds.

Nesting boxes provide safe places for raptors.

Some people are working to protect raptors. Governments pass laws. Some laws keep people from killing raptors. Other laws make it illegal to use chemicals that harm raptors.

People can make nesting boxes for raptors that have lost their habitat. Sometimes the population of a species is dangerously low. People capture some of the birds. They raise and care for the raptors. Then they release some of the offspring into the wild.

Raptors are important for a healthy world. They are also fun to watch soaring in the skies. There are many ways people can help protect these amazing birds.

FUN FACT

One of a raptor's ears is higher than the other. This helps them figure out where a sound is coming from.

The word *raptor* means "to grab and carry off."

GLOSSARY

ecosystem (EE-koh-sis-tum) An ecosystem is all of the living and nonliving things in an area. Raptors can give scientists clues about the health of an ecosystem.

habitat (HAB-ih-tat) A habitat is a place with the right temperature, weather, food, and water for an animal to live. Some raptors are facing habitat loss.

offspring (AWF-spring) Offspring are the descendants of a living thing. Some rodents have many offspring in one year.

pest (PEST) A pest is an animal that causes problems for humans. Rats and pocket gophers can become pests when living close to humans.

prey (PRAY) Prey are animals that other animals hunt and eat. Barn owls hunt for prey at night.

remains (reh-MAYNZ) Remains are dead bodies. Some raptors eat animal remains.

species (SPEE-sheez) A species is a specific group of animals that has the same features. The barn owl is one species of owl.

talons (TAL-uhns) Talons are sharp, hooked claws on a bird's feet. Raptors use their talons to catch and hold prey.

BOOKS

Curtis, Jennifer Keats. *Raptor Centers*. Mount Pleasant, SC: Arbordale Publishing, 2015.

Llewellyn, Claire. *Birds of Prey*. New York, NY: Kingfisher, 2017.

Spalding, Maddie. *The Animal Life Cycle*. Mankato, MN: The Child's World, 2019.

WEBSITES

Visit our website for links about raptors:
childsworld.com/links

Note to Parents, Teachers, and Librarians: We routinely verify our Web links to make sure they are safe and active sites. So encourage your readers to check them out!

INDEX

barn owl, 4–7, 10

chemicals, 16–19

ecosystem, 7, 11, 15

food web, 15

habitat, 16–19

nesting boxes, 19
nocturnal, 7

offspring, 11, 19

pests, 10, 11, 16
prey, 4, 8, 10, 12

remains, 12

species, 8, 11, 19

talons, 4, 8
turkey vultures, 12

vultures, 7, 12